McGRAW•HILL

HEALTH

PRACTICE WORKBOOK•GRADE 5

**McGraw-Hill
School Division**

New York   Farmington

McGraw-Hill School Division

A Division of The McGraw-Hill Companies

Copyright © 1999 McGraw-Hill School Division, a Division of the Educational and
Professional Publishing Group of The McGraw-Hill Companies, Inc.

McGraw-Hill School Division
1221 Avenue of the Americas
New York, New York 10020

Printed in the United States of America
ISBN 0-02-276875-0 / 5
1 2 3 4 5 6 7 8 9 045 03 02 01 00 99 98 97

Contents

WHAT IS HEALTH? 1

PERSONAL HEALTH CARE 2

ORAL HEALTH 3

EYE CARE 4

EAR CARE 5

SKIN, HAIR, AND NAIL CARE 6

STAGES OF LIFE 7

THE BODY—FROM CELLS TO SYSTEMS 8

YOUR BONES AND MUSCLES 9

YOUR HEART AND LUNGS 10

THE DIGESTIVE AND EXCRETORY SYSTEMS 11

THE NERVOUS AND ENDOCRINE SYSTEMS 12

WHAT IS SELF-ESTEEM? 13

EXPRESSING EMOTIONS 14

MANAGING STRESS 15

HEALTHY FAMILY LIFE 16

BUILDING HEALTHY RELATIONSHIPS 17

PEER AND CLASSROOM RELATIONSHIPS 18

ATTITUDES AND RELATIONSHIPS 19

NUTRIENTS AND YOUR HEALTH 20

FOOD GUIDE PYRAMID 21

MAKING FOOD CHOICES 22

FOOD LABELING 23

FOOD SAFETY HABITS 24

EATING HABITS AND YOUR HEALTH 25

THE IMPORTANCE OF PHYSICAL FITNESS 26

FITNESS SKILLS 27

TYPES OF PHYSICAL ACTIVITY 28

A PHYSICAL ACTIVITY PLAN 29

PHYSICAL ACTIVITY AND SAFETY 30

LEARNING ABOUT DISEASES 31

Communicable Diseases 32

The Immune System 33

HIV and AIDS 34

Noncommunicable Diseases 35

Staying Healthy 36

Legal Drugs and Illegal Drugs 37

Drug Dependence 38

Tobacco and Health 39

Tobacco and Social Issues 40

Alcohol and the Family 41

Marijuana and Other Drugs 42

Narcotics and Hallucinogens 43

Injury Prevention 44

Violence Prevention 45

Indoor Safety 46

Fire Safety 47

Outdoor Safety 48

Emergencies and First Aid 49

Community Health Care 50

Public Health Laws and Services 51

Air and Noise Pollution 52

Land and Water Pollution 53

Name: _____   Date: _____

WHAT IS HEALTH?

Complete each sentence with a word from the box. You may use a word more than once.

physical	emotional	intellectual	social

1. Eating well and being physically active is taking care of your
   _____ health.

2. You maintain your _____ health when you make and keep
   friends.

3. Working in groups and getting along with others can improve your
   _____ health.

4. Expressing your feelings helps maintain your _____ health.

5. Learning new things is part of good _____ health.

6. Respecting yourself is part of good _____ health.

Answer each question with complete sentences.

7. What are the three parts of health?

   _____

8. Why can't you control every aspect of your health?

   _____

9. What are two signs that a person is emotionally and intellectually
   healthy?

   _____

10. What would you do before following any advice about your health?

    _____

    _____

Name: _____ Date: _____

PERSONAL HEALTH CARE

Write True or False for each statement. If the statement is false, change the underlined word or phrase to make it true.

_____ 1. Responsibility for your health belongs mostly to your family.

_____ 2. When you look neat and smell fresh, you improve your emotional and social health.

_____ 3. During stage 1 of sleep, your muscles slowly relax.

_____ 4. Body temperature and blood pressure rise during stage 3 of sleep.

_____ 5. Medical and dental records can provide useful information about your medical history.

Write the word or phrase from the box that best completes each sentence.

```
once a year    twice a year    10–11 hours
        90 minutes        5–15 minutes
```

6. For the health of your teeth, you should have a dental checkup at least

   _____ .

7. To be well rested, most young people need about _____ of

   sleep a day.

8. During a night's sleep, each REM period lasts about _____ .

9. To maintain your health, it is a good idea to have a medical checkup at least

   _____ .

10. You enter the REM stage about _____ after you fall asleep.

Grade 5, Chapter 1, Lesson 2

Name: _____   Date: _____

ORAL HEALTH

Underline the phrase that best completes each sentence.

1. By the time you have reached the age of 21, you will probably have (32, 24) teeth.

2. Your teeth play an important part in the (digestive, breathing) process.

3. To bite off a piece of celery for a snack, you most likely use your (molars, incisors).

4. The white, protective outer layer of a tooth is the (crown, enamel).

5. It's best to floss (when food gets stuck between your teeth, at least once a day).

6. The (gum, pulp) surrounds each tooth and helps keep it in place.

7. (Pyorrhea, Caries) is a kind of tooth decay that produces small holes in the teeth.

8. An orthodontist might use (braces, root canal therapy) to correct malocclusion.

Answer each question with complete sentences.

9. What is the difference between the root and the crown of a tooth?

_____

_____

10. Why would a dentist use a cap or a bridge to repair teeth?

_____

_____

_____

Name: _____   Date: _____

EYE CARE

Complete each sentence with a word or words from the box.

| iris | cone cells | conjunctiva |
| ophthalmologist | optic nerve | rod cells |

1. The colored portion of the eye that controls the amount of light coming in

   is the _____.

2. The color of light is sensed by _____.

3. The brightness of light is sensed by _____.

4. The _____ connects your eye to your brain.

5. The sensitive lining of the eyelid is the _____.

6. An _____ examines eyes and can prescribe medicine,

   glasses, contact lenses, or surgery.

Match the word or words in Column A with the description in Column B.
Write the correct letter in the blank.

Column A

_____ 7. astigmatism

_____ 8. conjunctivitis

_____ 9. farsightedness

_____ 10. nearsightedness

Column B

A. pink eye that results when eyelid lining becomes infected

B. lengthening of eyeball makes it difficult to focus on distant objects

C. blurred vision caused by irregularly shaped cornea or lens

D. shortening of eyeball makes it difficult to focus on nearby objects

Grade 5, Chapter 1, Lesson 4

Name: _____   Date: _____

EAR CARE

Write True or False for each statement. If false, change the underlined word or phrase to make it true.

_____ 1. Three bones in the middle ear are the hammer, anvil, and <u>cochlea</u>.

_____ 2. The outer part of the ear canal is lined with fine hairs and <u>wax-producing glands</u>.

_____ 3. The <u>auricle</u> separates the outer ear from the middle ear.

_____ 4. An audiologist <u>prescribes medicine for ear infections</u>.

_____ 5. Exposure to <u>very loud noise</u> can cause permanent hearing loss.

Choose a word or phrase from the box to label each part of the diagram.

| auditory nerve | cochlea | ear canal | eardrum | sound waves |

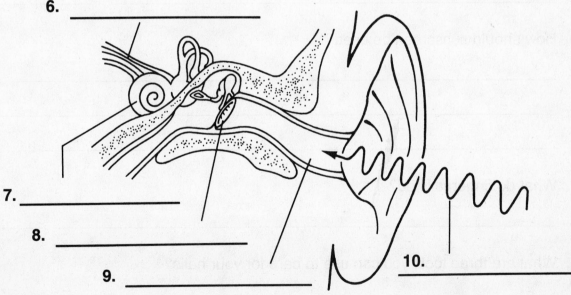

6. _____

7. _____

8. _____

9. _____

10. _____

Name: _____   Date: _____

SKIN, HAIR, AND NAIL CARE

Underline the phrase that best completes each sentence.

1. (Cells, Pores) are the smallest living parts of the body.

2. Hair and nails are a thickened form of (fatty tissue, epidermis).

3. (Acne, Athlete's foot) is a skin infection caused by a fungus.

4. The higher the SPF, the more protection you have against (harmful sun rays, insect bites).

5. Sharing combs or brushes is not a good idea because it spreads (head lice, dandruff).

6. The special skin that surrounds the nails of your fingers and toes is called the (follicle, cuticle).

Answer each question with complete sentences.

7. What are pimples and what produces them?

_____

_____

8. How should sunscreen be used?

_____

_____

_____

9. What do fingernails do?

_____

10. What are three tools you can use to care for your nails?

_____

Name: _____   Date: _____

STAGES OF LIFE

Write the word or phrase from the box that best completes each sentence.

adolescence	childhood	environment	health practices	traits

1. During _____ you learn many good health habits, such as keeping clean, eating well, and brushing your teeth.

2. A period of rapid growth is very common during _____.

3. Many of your characteristics, or _____, were inherited from your parents.

4. The air you breathe is part of your _____.

5. Eating a balanced diet and getting plenty of rest are good _____.

Write True or False for each statement. If false, change the underlined word or phrase to make it true.

_____ 6. It is very unusual for a growth spurt to happen during a person's adolescence.

_____ 7. As an adolescent, the number and difficulty of your tasks at home and at school will probably increase.

_____ 8. Both heredity and environment play a part in your growth and development.

_____ 9. You did not choose your inherited traits.

_____ 10. Infancy is a time of slow growth and development.

Name: _____   Date: _____

THE BODY—FROM CELLS TO SYSTEMS

Write the word or phrase from the box that matches each picture.

cell	body system	organ

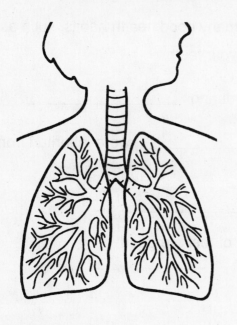

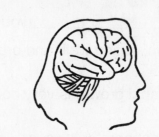

2. _____

1. _____   3. _____

Underline the phrase that best completes each sentence.

4. The growth and division of cells occurs at a (rapid, slow) rate.

5. A basic job of cells is to take in (carbon dioxide, oxygen).

6. (Nerve cells, skin cells) bring messages from your eyes to your brain.

7. The brain is made up largely of (muscle, nerve) tissue.

8. A (tissue, organ) is a group of similar cells that work together to do a job.

9. The stomach and intestines are part of the (skeletal, digestive) body

   system.

10. (Cells, Hearts) are the basic structural units of living things.

McGraw-Hill School Division

Name: _____   Date: _____

YOUR BONES AND MUSCLES

Write the word or phrase from the box that matches each pictured body part.

| contracted muscle   hinge joint   relaxed muscle   tendon |

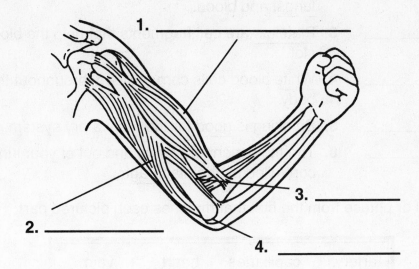

1. _____

2. _____

3. _____

4. _____

Underline the phrase that best completes each sentence.

5. The human body contains about (100, 200) bones.

6. The bones of the body support your weight, enable you to move, and protect your (internal organs, skin).

7. Immovable joints are found in the (elbow, skull).

8. The ends of some bones are protected by flexible tissue called (cartilage, ligaments).

9. Heart muscle is an example of (involuntary muscle, voluntary muscle).

10. Special care for sprains is called "RICE", which is the abbreviation for Rest, Ice, Compression, and (Elevation, Exercise).

Name: _____   Date: _____

YOUR HEART AND LUNGS

Write True or False for each statement. If false, change the underlined word or phrase to make it true.

_____ 1. The circulatory system <u>gets rid of</u> oxygen, food, and other materials throughout the body.

_____ 2. The circulatory system is made up of the heart, <u>lungs</u>, and blood.

_____ 3. <u>Platelets</u> are cell fragments that help the blood to clot.

_____ 4. <u>White</u> blood cells carry oxygen throughout the body.

_____ 5. Smoking is <u>good</u> for the respiratory system.

_____ 6. The movement of air into and out of your lungs is controlled by the <u>diaphragm</u>.

Write the word or phrase from the box that matches each pictured part.

artery	capillaries	heart	vein

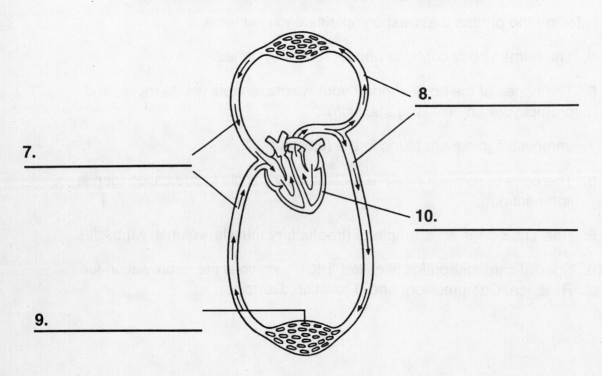

7. _____

8. _____

9. _____

10. _____

McGraw-Hill School Division

Name: _____   Date: _____

THE DIGESTIVE AND EXCRETORY SYSTEMS

Circle the letter of the best answer.

1. The most important job of the digestive system is to
   a. get food and oxygen to your cells
   b. change food into a form that cells can use
   c. get rid of wastes

2. When you swallow food, it enters a tube called the
   a. esophagus   b. intestine   c. pancreas

3. Digestive juices that help break down food are found in your
   a. lungs   b. heart and pancreas   c. stomach and small intestine

4. A good way to take care of your digestive system is to eat food with a lot of
   a. fiber   b. fat   c. water

5. A substance produced by your liver to aid digestion is
   a. bile   b. villi   c. saliva

6. Undigested food passes into the
   a. bloodstream   b. capillaries   c. large intestine

Underline the phrase that best completes each sentence.

7. Digestion first begins in the (mouth, stomach).

8. Villi are tiny finger-like projections that line the (small intestine, stomach).

9. Tiny filters in the kidneys help to remove (wastes, oxygen) from the blood.

10. Organs of the excretory system are the kidneys and (liver, skin).

Name: _____   Date: _____

THE NERVOUS AND ENDOCRINE SYSTEMS

Write True or False for each statement. If false, change the underlined word or phrase to make it true.

_____ **1.** The nervous system is made up of your brain, spinal cord, and nerves.

_____ **2.** Sensory neurons relay messages to the brain.

_____ **3.** The cerebrum controls the muscle coordination and balance.

_____ **4.** The deepening of boys' voices at puberty is an example of a secondary sex characteristic.

_____ **5.** The endocrine system controls the body with chemical messengers called neurons.

_____ **6.** The pituitary gland controls the growth of bones and muscles as well as the action of other glands of the endocrine system.

Write the word or phrase from the box that best completes each sentence.

```
cerebrum    motor neurons    medulla    puberty
```

7. Nerves that relay messages to muscles are called _____.

8. The part of the brain that takes up about two thirds of it is the

_____.

9. The part of the brain that controls involuntary acts, such as breathing, is the

_____.

10. The pituitary gland sends out a hormone that triggers a growth spurt during

_____.

Name: _____   Date: _____

WHAT IS SELF-ESTEEM?

Write True or False for each statement. If false, change the underlined word or phrase to make it true.

_____   **1.** Talents and abilities that make us proud of ourselves are our underlined weaknesses.

_____   **2.** The qualities that make you different from everyone else are part of your personality.

_____   **3.** If you have a good opinion of yourself, you will have a positive self-concept.

_____   **4.** People with high self-esteem often get bored.

Write the word or phrase that best completes each sentence.

5. A person's basic physical needs include food, shelter, water, and

_____ .

6. You can build your self-esteem by choosing friends that have

_____ self-esteem.

7. An example of a health professional who can help rebuild a person's self-esteem is a _____ .

Answer each question with complete sentences.

8. What are two basic emotional needs that people have?

_____

9. How can knowing your strengths help build your self-esteem?

_____

_____

10. What are some signs that a person may need help rebuilding his or her self-esteem?

_____

_____

Name: _____   Date: _____

EXPRESSING EMOTIONS

Write the word from the box that matches each picture.

anger	fear	joy	sadness	sympathy	worry

1. _____ 2. _____ 3. _____

4. _____ 5. _____ 6. _____

Answer each question with complete sentences.

7. How does expressing your emotions help your social health?

_____

8. What can you do if you think a conflict arose because of something you said?

_____

9. Who can help you resolve a conflict when nothing else seems to work?

_____

10. How can many misunderstandings be avoided?

_____

Name: _____   Date: _____

MANAGING STRESS

Here are five sentences about managing stress. Put a check mark in the blank beside each sentence that gives you good advice about dealing with stress or stressful situations. Then use complete sentences to explain why the advice is good or why it is not.

_____ 1. Lie down, close your eyes, and relax by listening to some soothing music or by pretending you're in a quiet place.

_____

_____

_____ 2. Don't worry about eating healthful foods or getting plenty of rest and sleep.

_____

_____

_____ 3. Talk about your feelings with family members, friends, counselors, teachers, or other people you trust.

_____

_____

_____ 4. Take a long walk or try some physical activity.

_____

_____

_____ 5. Decide what to do about the stressful situation right away and take immediate action.

_____

_____

Name: _____ Date: _____

HEALTHY FAMILY LIFE

Match the word or words in Column A with the description in Column B.
Write the correct letter in the blank.

Column A	Column B
_____ 1. extended family	**A.** a family adopts and raises children born to others
_____ 2. single-parent family	
_____ 3. adoptive family	**B.** family includes other relatives who might act as parents
_____ 4. nuclear family	
_____ 5. blended family	**C.** one or both parents have been married before; may include children from a previous marriage
	D. one parent raises children
	E. two parents raise children

Write <u>True</u> or <u>False</u> for each statement. If false, change the underlined word or phrase to make it true.

_____ 6. It's <u>unusual</u> for family members to argue sometimes.

_____ 7. In a healthy family, members try to communicate, show support, <u>cooperate</u>, and settle differences.

_____ 8. When you are dependable, it means that others <u>cannot</u> count on you.

_____ 9. A <u>foster</u> family cares temporarily for one or more children born to others.

Write complete sentences to answer the question.

10. How is a *privilege* different from a *right*?

_____

_____

Name: _____   Date: _____

BUILDING HEALTHY RELATIONSHIPS

Underline the phrase that best completes each sentence.

1. A friend is someone who (ignores, understands) your feelings.

2. When trying to straighten things out with a friend, begin your sentences with (I, you).

3. A friend that joins a clique and leaves you out is acting in (a friendly, an unfriendly) way.

4. A friend fails to respect your feelings and beliefs over and over again. It is most likely time (to have an argument, to end the friendship).

5. Crying is an infant's way of (communicating with, annoying) people.

Answer each question in complete sentences.

6. What is one way you could meet new friends?

_____

7. What does it mean to appreciate a friend?

_____

8. Why are friends usually willing to compromise when there's a problem?

_____

9. What can you do when a friend acts unfriendly?

_____

_____

10. When you're around very young children, why should you pay careful attention to them?

_____

_____

Name: _____   Date: _____

PEER AND CLASSROOM RELATIONSHIPS

Write True or False for each statement. If false, change the underlined word or phrase to make it true.

_____ 1. When friends try to convince you to recycle, they are putting <u>positive</u> peer pressure on you.

_____ 2. Taking a stand against negative peer pressure is <u>never</u> difficult.

_____ 3. When friends pressure you to do something unhealthful, you <u>should</u> go along with them.

_____ 4. A student carries out his or her role <u>by learning</u>.

_____ 5. During a fire drill, you should <u>follow</u> your teacher's directions.

Answer each question in complete sentences.

6. What is one way to avoid situations that might cause you problems?

_____

7. Why is cooperation important in an effective classroom?

_____

Look at the picture. What are three things that show this is an effective classroom?

8. _____

_____

9. _____

_____

10. _____

_____

Name: _____   Date: _____

ATTITUDES AND RELATIONSHIPS

A family from another country moves in next door to you. They have a child who is your age and who will be in your class. The family members dress in their native clothing and have customs that are very different from yours.

Use a word from the box to identify each kind of attitude described below. Then use complete sentences to explain your answers.

intolerance	prejudice	bossiness	stereotype	tolerance

1. You decide to welcome the new family, make friends with the child, and try to learn more about their culture.

   _____

   _____

2. When your new neighbor comes to school the next day, the other kids in your class start making fun of how he looks and dresses.

   _____

   _____

3. A classmate says that *all* people from your neighbor's country dress weirdly.

   _____

   _____

4. A classmate is impolite to your new friend, though she doesn't know him. She says, "Those people don't deserve respect."

   _____

   _____

5. The leader of your after-school club never listens to your suggestions and gets angry when you ask him to repeat something.

   _____

   _____

Name: _____ Date: _____

NUTRIENTS AND YOUR HEALTH

Write the word from the box that best completes each sentence.

calorie	carbohydrates	nutrients	proteins	vitamins

1. Substances in food that are needed to maintain health are

   _____ .

2. A unit that is used to measure the amount of energy in food is a

   _____ .

3. Nutrients that the body needs in small amounts to grow and function

   well are _____ .

4. Nutrients that provide materials for growth, maintenance, and repair

   of cells are _____ .

5. Nutrients that are the body's main source of energy are

   _____ .

Write True or False for each statement. If false, change the underlined
word or phrase to make it true.

_____ 6. There is no single "perfect" food that will give
you all the underlined nutrients your body needs.

_____ 7. Sugar and starches are two main kinds of
underlined proteins.

_____ 8. underlined Minerals are nutrients that the body needs in
small amounts to control body processes
and build new cells.

_____ 9. People can live only a few days without underlined food.

_____ 10. Anemia is a disease that may result from a
diet with too little of the mineral underlined iron.

Name: _____   Date: _____

FOOD GUIDE PYRAMID

Write the word or phrase from the box that best completes each sentence.

balanced diet	food groups
Food Guide Pyramid	recommended serving

1. Groups made up of foods that contain similar amounts of important nutrients are _____ .

2. The _____ is a diagram that provides information about food groups and healthful daily servings from each group.

3. A _____ is a suggested amount of food to eat to maintain a healthy diet.

4. A _____ is a diet, maintained over time, that includes a variety of foods that provide nutrition in moderate amounts.

Underline the word or phrase that best completes each sentence.

5. Fats, oils, and sweets should be used (often, sparingly).

6. The Bread, Cereal, Rice, and Pasta Group includes foods from (animals, grains).

7. Eating a balanced meal (is, is not) the same as having a balanced diet).

8. Fats, oils, and sweets have many calories and (few, many) nutrients.

9. A good source of fiber is the (Milk, Yogurt, Cheese Group; Vegetable Group).

10. The Bread, Cereal, Rice, and Pasta Group is a good source of (carbohydrates, fats).

McGraw-Hill School Division

Name: _____   Date: _____

MAKING FOOD CHOICES

Write True or False for each statement. If false, change the underlined word or phrase to make it true.

_____ 1. Availability of food at certain times of the year may be a factor that influences your food choices.

_____ 2. Keep your weight at a healthy level by balancing your food intake with diets.

_____ 3. Too much sugar can also lead to tooth decay.

_____ 4. Excess sugar is stored as body muscle.

_____ 5. No more than 30% (1/3) of your daily calories should come from fats.

_____ 6. Vitamins make the body store excess fluid which may result in weight gain and an increase in blood pressure.

_____ 7. "Reduced Fat" foods may have less fat than the original product, but they may still have many calories and a high fat content.

Write the word from the box that best completes each sentence.

```
┌──────────────────────────────────────────────────────────┐
│   media        saturated fat        unsaturated fat        │
└──────────────────────────────────────────────────────────┘
```

8. A kind of fat, such as corn oil, most often made from plant-based foods is an _____ .

9. The _____ are forms of communication that reach a large audience.

10. A _____ is a kind of fat most often found in animal-based foods such as meat, cheese, and egg yolks.

Name: _____   Date: _____

FOOD LABELING

Write the word or phrase from the box that best completes each sentence.

additive	ingredients	perishable	preservative	processed foods

1. An additive to keep food from spoiling is a _____.

2. Substances that are mixed together to make foods are _____.

3. Foods to which substances have been added during canning,

   freezing, or drying them are _____.

4. Foods that are likely to spoil are _____.

5. An ingredient added to packaged food to improve its nutrient content

   is an _____.

Read the food label. Then underline the word that completes each sentence.

Nutrition Facts
Serving Size 1

Calories	80
	% DV*
Fat 0g	0%
Cholesterol 0mg	0%
Sodium 230mg	10%
Total Carb. 18g	6%
Fiber 1g	4%
Sugars 2g	
Protein 1g	

Vitamin A	10%	Vitamin C	15%
Calcium	0%	Iron	30%
Vitamin D	8%	Thiamin	15%

* Percent Daily Values (DV) are based
on a 2,000 calorie diet.

Ingredients: Milled corn, sugar, salt,
malt flavoring, high fructose corn syrup,
ascorbic acid (vitamin C)

6. The number of servings is (1, 21).

7. The number of calories in one serving
   is (0, 80).

8. One serving of the product gives you
   (less, more) than the total Daily Value
   of sodium.

9. The nutrient with the highest Percent
   Daily Value is (iron, vitamin C).

10. There is more (corn syrup, milled corn)
    than any other ingredient.

Name: _____ Date: _____

FOOD SAFETY HABITS

Write the word or phrase from the box that best completes each sentence.

| botulism | contamination | food poisoning | Salmonella |

1. A kind of bacteria that causes illness is _____.

2. Spoilage caused by unclean conditions is _____.

3. Food poisoning caused by toxins, or poisons, produced by certain bacteria is _____.

4. An illness caused by eating spoiled foods is

   _____.

Write True or False for each statement. If false, change the underlined word or phrase to make it true.

_____ 5. Salmonella are bacteria that grow on <u>uncooked</u> eggs and some meats.

_____ 6. Botulism is a rare illness that comes from <u>food</u> that has spoiled in a can or other container.

_____ 7. You can leave leftovers at room temperature for no more than <u>five</u> hours.

_____ 8. Buying food <u>before</u> its expiration date increases the risk of getting food that is spoiled.

_____ 9. You should keep refrigerated food at <u>a temperature of 40°F</u> or lower.

_____ 10. Sometimes, bacteria from one food item spoils other foods that are placed on the same <u>surface</u>.

Grade 5, Chapter 5, Lesson 5

McGraw-Hill School Division

Name: _____   Date: _____

EATING HABITS AND YOUR HEALTH

Underline the word or phrase that best completes each sentence.

1. The key to maintaining a healthful body weight is to (burn up, store) the calories you take in from the food you eat.

2. Government guidelines state that boys and girls your age need between (220 and 250, 2200 and 2500) calories a day.

3. Sitting quietly uses (fewer, more) calories than jogging for the same amount of time.

4. Fad diets are usually unhealthful because they (limit people to eating certain foods, let people eat all types of food).

5. Stress and (low self-esteem, a positive attitude) may result in poor eating habits.

Write the word or phrase from the box that best completes each sentence.

anorexia nervosa	bulimia	caloric expenditure	caloric intake	fad diet

6. The calories a person burns up is _____.

7. An eating disorder in which a person eats large amounts of food in a short time and then vomits on purpose is _____.

8. A weight-loss diet that is popular and usually unhealthful is called a _____.

9. The number of calories a person consumes is called _____.

10. An eating disorder in which a person has an unrealistic fear of becoming overweight and eats very little is _____.

Name: _____   Date: _____

THE IMPORTANCE OF PHYSICAL FITNESS

Write the word from the box that best completes each sentence.

```
strength        body composition        posture

        endurance              flexibility
```

1. You can increase your _____ by doing exercises that stretch your muscles and work your joints.

2. The amount of the body's fat tissue in relation to lean tissue is

   _____ .

3. Lifting a heavy box requires _____ .

4. Sitting erect in a chair or standing up straight are examples of good

   _____ .

5. The ability of your heart and lungs to keep you physically active without

   getting tired is called heart and lung _____ .

Write True or False for each statement. If false, change the underlined word or phrase to make it true.

_____ 6. Regular exercise can help you increase your resting heart rate.

_____ 7. Exercise can help your lungs get rid of more carbon dioxide.

_____ 8. To be healthy, your body needs no fat.

_____ 9. Working on physical fitness goals can help us make new friends.

_____ 10. Being physically fit helps produce stress.

Name: _____   Date: _____

FITNESS SKILLS

Underline the phrase that best completes each sentence.

1. Good (coordination, balance) helps your eyes work with your arm muscles when you throw a ball.

2. People who (remain physically active, avoid exercise) have better health.

3. Walking slowly through a tricky obstacle course can help you develop your (speed, agility)

4. You can improve your power by (jumping up and down, playing tug-of-war with a partner).

Write the word or words from the box that matches each pictured activity.

| agility | balance | coordination | power | speed | reaction time |

5.

_____

6.

_____

7.

_____

8.

_____

9.

_____

10.

_____

McGraw-Hill School Division

Name: _____   Date: _____

TYPES OF PHYSICAL ACTIVITY

Complete each sentence with a word from the box. One word will be used twice.

isometric	isotonic
aerobic	anaerobic

1. A push-up is an example of an _____ exercise because it uses muscle contraction and movement to build strength.

2. An _____ exercise uses up more oxygen than your heart and lungs can provide.

3. Jogging, in-line skating, and jumping rope are all examples of _____ exercises.

4. Pressing your hands against a door frame is an example of an _____ exercise because it builds strength using very little body movement.

5. An _____ exercise should be done briskly for about 20 to 30 minutes.

Write True or False for each statement. If false, change the underlined word or phrase to make it true.

_____ 6. Isometric exercises cannot increase muscle strength.

_____ 7. Aerobic exercise should be done at a medium or moderately fast pace.

_____ 8. An anaerobic exercise should be done for at least 20 minutes.

_____ 9. You should begin a workout with a rapid aerobic exercise.

_____ 10. Cool-down exercises can be a fast version of the workout exercise you were doing.

McGraw-Hill School Division

Name: _____   Date: _____

A PHYSICAL ACTIVITY PLAN

Here are some sentences about designing a physical activity plan. Put a check mark in the blank beside each sentence that gives you good advice about fitness. Then explain why each sentence is or is not good advice. Use complete sentences.

_____ **1.** It is impossible to measure how fit a person is.

_____

_____

_____

_____ **2.** A good fitness program should include a variety of activities instead of just one.

_____

_____

_____

_____ **3.** Warm-up exercises are only necessary if you are working out for more than 45 minutes.

_____

_____

_____

_____ **4.** A health journal can be a helpful fitness tool.

_____

_____

_____

_____ **5.** It doesn't matter how often you exercise, so long as you exercise energetically when you do.

_____

_____

_____

McGraw-Hill School Division

Name: _____   Date: _____

PHYSICAL ACTIVITY AND SAFETY

Complete each sentence with a word from the box.

blisters	safety equipment	flexible
	injury	layers

1. When dressing for outdoor activities in cold weather, you should dress in

   _____ .

2. Harm or damage to a person or thing is an _____ .

3. Helmets and kneepads are types of _____ .

4. Some kneepads, such as those used by volleyball players, should be soft

   and _____ .

5. Cotton socks can be worn to cushion your feet and reduce

   _____ .

Write True or False for each statement. If false, change the underlined word or phrase to make it true.

_____ 6. Water is the best thing to drink while exercising.

_____ 7. Your exercise clothing should be loose enough to let you move freely.

_____ 8. Rapid, high-energy exercises can help prevent injury and soreness in your muscles.

_____ 9. Broken sporting equipment will protect you as well as new equipment.

_____ 10. After exercise, your muscles should feel worse than they did before you started.

McGraw-Hill School Division

Name: _____   Date: _____

LEARNING ABOUT DISEASES

Write the word from the box that best completes each sentence.

communicable disease	host	disease
noncommunicable disease	microbes	viruses

1. A breakdown in the way the body works is a _____ .

2. A disease that cannot be passed from person to person is a

   _____ .

3. A disease that is caused by microbes that invade the body is a

   _____ .

4. Microbes that can only reproduce inside living cells are

   _____ .

5. Antiseptics and antibacterial soaps kill _____ or keep

   them from growing.

6. The place that provides the environment in which microbes can live and

   reproduce is a _____ .

Write True or False for each statement. If false, change the underlined word or phrase to make it true.

_____ 7. A noncommunicable disease may be caused by
   heredity.

_____ 8. As a virus uses substances in a cell to reproduce, it
   often helps the cell it has infected.

_____ 9. Athlete's foot is a disease caused by a virus.

_____ 10. Microbes are carried into the air when an infected
   person sneezes or coughs.

Name: _____   Date: _____

COMMUNICABLE DISEASES

Write the word or phrase from the box that best completes each sentence.

| antibiotics   incubation |
| influenza   symptom   vaccine |
---

1. A communicable disease starts with an _____ period, before a person is even aware of being ill.

2. An indication of a disease is a _____.

3. Viruses cause the respiratory disease called _____.

4. A substance made from dead or weakened microbes that is injected or swallowed to protect the body against a specific disease is a

   _____.

5. Medicines that can kill bacteria are _____.

Underline the phrase that best completes each sentence.

6. During the (convalescent, peak) period of a communicable disease, you are recovering from the disease.

7. Influenza symptoms are similar to (cold, tetanus) symptoms—but worse.

8. Needle inoculation means you receive MMR and DPT vaccines by (injection, swallowing it).

9. To make vaccines, viruses are often grown on animal (tissue, waste products) in laboratories.

10. Washing hands, keeping flies away from food, and separating sick patients are changes in (behavior, heredity) that have helped to reduce diseases.

McGraw-Hill School Division

Name: _____   Date: _____

THE IMMUNE SYSTEM

Write the word or phrase from the box that best completes each sentence.

antibody	fever	immune system
immunity	white blood cells	

1. A raised body temperature — 99.6°F (37.7°C) or higher — is a
   _____.

2. All of the parts and functions of your body that fight disease-causing
   microbes make up your body's _____ .

3. A chemical made by the body that helps destroy or weaken bacteria,
   viruses, and other microbes is an _____.

4. Large blood cells that help the body fight disease are
   _____.

5. The protection against or ability to fight disease is _____.

Write True or False for each statement. If false, change the underlined
word or phrase to make it true.

_____ 6. Your skin is the first line of defense to keep
disease-causing microbes from entering
your body.

_____ 7. Your windpipe and all other air passages are
filled with cilia that constantly sweep
downward to prevent bacteria from entering
the lungs.

_____ 8. Red blood cells stop the spread of disease
by surrounding microbes that enter the body.

_____ 9. If you have immunity to a disease, you
probably will get the disease again.

_____ 10. A vaccine contains a weakened or dead form
of a microbe that is not strong enough to
cause the disease, but is strong enough to
stimulate the production of an antibody.

Name: _____   Date: _____

HIV AND AIDS

Write True or False for each statement. If false, change the underlined word or phrase to make it true.

_____ **1.** HIV is a virus that causes a deficiency in the underline{nervous} system.

_____ **2.** People with AIDS often become ill with tuberculosis or a very unusual type of underline{skin cancer}.

_____ **3.** HIV underline{is} spread through casual contact.

_____ **4.** Sexual contact is a underline{risk factor} for transmitting HIV.

_____ **5.** HIV underline{can} be passed from the infected blood of an injured person.

Write the word or phrase from the box that best completes each sentence.

abstinence	AIDS	HIV
risk factor		syndrome

6. A virus that causes a deficiency in the immune system and leads to AIDS is _____.

7. The act of avoiding a behavior completely is _____ .

8. A group of symptoms that occur together in a particular disease is a _____.

9. A very serious disease in which the immune system is extremely weak is _____.

10. A trait or behavior that increases a person's chances of getting a disease is a _____.

Name: _____ Date: _____

NONCOMMUNICABLE DISEASES

Underline the word or phrase that best completes each sentence.

1. One treatment of cancer is radiation, which uses (a form of high energy X-rays, very strong drugs) to kill cancer cells.

2. The leading cause of death in the United States is (cancer, heart disease).

3. If blood flow to the brain is blocked, a person may suffer a (heart attack, stroke).

4. Sickle cell anemia is a disease caused by (behavior, heredity).

5. Sunscreens help to protect you from (lung, skin) cancer.

Answer each question in complete sentences.

6. What causes noncommunicable diseases?

_____

_____

7. What is a chronic disease?

_____

_____

8. What is a degenerative disease?

_____

9. What is cancer?

_____

_____

10. What is a disease that is related to smoking?

_____

McGraw-Hill School Division

Name: _____   Date: _____

STAYING HEALTHY

Label each pictured lifestyle choice that helps you stay healthy.

1.

_____

2.

_____

3.

_____

4.

_____

Write True or False for each statement. If false, change the underlined word or phrase to make it true.

_____ 5. A lifestyle choice is a decision that affects the kind of life you live.

_____ 6. Smoking is a healthy lifestyle choice.

_____ 7. Resistance is your body's ability to fight off a disease.

_____ 8. Staying relaxed seems to have a good effect on the immune system.

_____ 9. Dieticians are responsible for preparing medicines that have been prescribed.

_____ 10. A food inspector makes sure that food is safe to eat.

Name: _____   Date: _____

LEGAL DRUGS AND ILLEGAL DRUGS

Write <u>True</u> or <u>False</u> for each statement. If false, change the underlined word or phrase to make it true.

_____ 1. Drugs <u>cannot</u> do serious harm to your health.

_____ 2. <u>Over-the counter</u> drugs can be purchased without a doctor's prescription.

_____ 3. <u>Only illegal</u> drugs can have side effects.

_____ 4. Illegal drugs may affect your <u>heart rate, blood pressure, and nervous system.</u>

_____ 5. If a medicine is not working, you should <u>take twice the recommended dosage.</u>

Underline the phrase that best completes each sentence.

6. You must always get a doctor's written order when you need a (prescription, non-prescription) drug.

7. Alcohol and tobacco are examples of legal drugs that are not (dangerous, medicines).

8. The careless or improper use of a medicine or legal drug in a way that can harm you is (drug abuse, drug misuse).

9. The purposeful use of drugs in ways that can seriously harm your physical, emotional, intellectual, and social health is (drug abuse, drug misuse).

10. People who are caught with (over-the-counter, illegal) drugs can be sent to prison.

Name: _____   Date: _____

DRUG DEPENDENCE

Here are some sentences about drug dependence. Put a check mark in the blank beside each sentence that gives you good advice about drugs. Then explain why each sentence is or is not good advice. Use complete sentences.

_____ 1. Drug dependence can seriously harm a person's physical, intellectual and emotional, and social health.

_____

_____

_____

_____ 2. Peer pressure is usually harmless because your peers always want the same things you do.

_____

_____

_____ 3. You will never have to face the difficulties of withdrawal if you don't start taking drugs in the first place.

_____

_____

_____

_____ 4. Becoming an active member of your community is a good strategy for staying drug free.

_____

_____

_____ 5. When people have problems with drugs, they should try to solve their own problems without getting help from others.

_____

_____

_____

McGraw-Hill School Division

Name: _____   Date: _____

TOBACCO AND HEALTH

Underline the phrase that best completes each sentence.

1. The addictive drug in tobacco is (nicotine, carbon monoxide).

2. A substance that causes cancer is called a (poisonous gas, carcinogen).

3. Smoking increases the amount of (oxygen, carbon monoxide) in blood.

4. The (atherosclerosis, tar) in cigarette smoke contains many substances that are known to cause cancer.

5. Emphysema is a lung disease that prevents the body from getting enough (oxygen, nicotine).

Answer each question in complete sentences.

6. How does nicotine affect the heart?

    _____

    _____

7. What happens when carbon monoxide enters the blood?

    _____

8. How are smoking and cancer related?

    _____

Look at the picture. What are the benefits of staying tobacco free?

9. _____

    _____

    _____

    _____

10. _____

    _____

    _____

    _____

Name: _____   Date: _____

TOBACCO AND SOCIAL ISSUES

Here are some sentences about tobacco and social issues. Put a check mark in the blank beside each sentence that is true about smoking. Then explain why each sentence is or is not true. Use complete sentences.

_____ **1.** You can't be hurt by being with other people who smoke.

_____

_____

_____

_____ **2.** The Surgeon General has not found any evidence that smoking and cancer are related.

_____

_____

_____

_____ **3.** No-smoking laws help to keep public spaces safe and free of hazardous smoke.

_____

_____

_____ **4.** Cigarette advertisements are required to show you the problems that can result from smoking.

_____

_____

_____

_____ **5.** Passive smoke is a threat to the lives of both children and adults.

_____

_____

_____

McGraw-Hill School Division

40

Name: _____   Date: _____

ALCOHOL AND THE FAMILY

Write the word from the box that best completes each sentence.

sober	withdrawal	alcoholism	intoxication	cirrhosis

1. An addiction to alcohol is called _____.

2. Drinking alcohol can lead to _____, a condition in which a person's coordination and judgment can be damaged.

3. Alcoholics Anonymous is a group that helps people stay _____.

4. Once physical dependence has set in, a person who tries to stop drinking may suffer painful _____.

5. Liver damage may lead to_____, a life-threatening disease that destroys healthy cells in the liver.

Underline the phrase that best completes each sentence.

6. Alcohol (increases, decreases) a person's ability to think and solve problems.

7. The (liver, heart) does most of the work of breaking down alcohol.

8. Leading an alcohol-free lifestyle can increase your (level of intoxication, control of your body and mind).

Describe a response to both of the following situations.

9. A friend's older brother offers you a beer.

_____

10. Your neighbor is worried that her cousin has a drinking problem.

_____

_____

McGraw-Hill School Division

Name: _____ Date: _____

MARIJUANA AND OTHER DRUGS

Complete the definition of each word.

1. A stimulant is _____
_____

2. An inhalant is _____
_____

3. A depressant is _____
_____

4. Marijuana is _____
_____

5. An amphetamine is _____
_____

Write True or False for each statement. If false, change the underlined word or phrase to make it true.

_____ **6.** Marijuana interferes with the ability to think clearly.

_____ **7.** Cocaine, coffee, and diet pills are all types of depressants.

_____ **8.** All stimulants are highly addictive.

_____ **9.** Inhaling fumes from glue or paint thinner can strengthen muscles and appetite.

_____ **10.** Over-the-counter sleeping pills are never habit-forming.

Name: _____   Date: _____

NARCOTICS AND HALLUCINOGENS

Write the word from the box that best completes each sentence..

intravenous	HIV	hallucinogen
healthy		narcotics

1. A drug is _____ if the user injects it into the body with a needle.

2. A drug is a _____ if it makes the user see or hear things that are not really there.

3. Sharing needles can lead to the spread of the _____ virus.

4. Some drugs that are prescribed by doctors for sleep and to relieve pain are called _____.

5. Staying drug free can help you enjoy _____ relationships with family and friends.

Underline the phrase that best completes each sentence.

6. Heroin is an (illegal narcotic, legal amphetamine) that is very addictive and dangerous.

7. Withdrawal from heroin is very (quick and painless, difficult and painful).

8. People who use hallucinogens increase the risk of (lung or heart disease, accidents or overdose).

9. If your lifestyle choice is to remain drug free, you will be able to (act more violently, think clearly).

10. With a drug-free lifestyle, you most likely will take good care of yourself and have (high, low) self-esteem.

McGraw-Hill School Division

Name: _____   Date: _____

INJURY PREVENTION

Write the word from the box that best completes each sentence.

hazard	chemical	unintentional
intersection		overload

1. A condition that creates a risk of danger is a _____.

2. Never cross the street against a light at an _____.

3. Mixing two cleaners could cause a _____ hazard.

4. Physical harm that is not deliberate is an _____ injury.

5. You should be careful not to _____ electrical outlets.

Write Safe or Not Safe for each statement. If not safe, write a
related rule that is safe.

_____ 6. Wrap tape around frayed or worn cords and plugs.

_____

_____ 7. Always use a pot holder or a heat-resistant glove
     when handling items that have been in the oven.

_____

_____ 8. Be very careful when hopping onto moving tractors
     or pick-up trucks.

_____

_____ 9. If you see a hazard at school, report it to an adult.

_____

_____ 10. Always get in or out of a car on the driver's side.

_____

McGraw-Hill School Division

Name: _____ Date: _____

VIOLENCE PREVENTION

Here are some sentences about violence prevention. Put a check mark in the blank beside each sentence that gives you good advice about how to avoid violence. Then explain why each sentence is or is not good advice. Use complete sentences.

_____ **1.** Anger is a dangerous emotion, so you should never be angry.

_____

_____

_____ **2.** Even though it can seem like a quick solution, violence is never a positive solution to any problem.

_____

_____

_____ **3.** If someone acts violently toward you, you have no choice but to respond with violence.

_____

_____

_____ **4.** One good way to resolve a conflict is to stay calm and allow each person the chance to explain his or her side.

_____

_____

_____

_____ **5.** Compromises are only for situations that have already become violent.

_____

_____

_____

Name: _____   Date: _____

INDOOR SAFETY

Underline the phrase that best completes each sentence.

1. A (sprain, bruise) is an injury to a part of your body that does not break the skin but causes it to change color.

2. A (sprain, bruise) is an injury caused by the sudden overstretching of a muscle.

3. To prevent falls and slips, you should wear (rubber-soled, dress shoes) when walking on slippery surfaces.

4. If you are home alone, you should never (let a stranger into your house, answer the phone).

5. If someone is poisoned, you should try to (throw the poison container away right away, save the poison container).

Write the word from the box that best completes each sentence.

stranger	never	poison
always		emergency

6. You should _____ wipe up spilled liquids right away.

7. Never tell a _____ your name, address, or phone number.

8. A _____ is a substance that is harmful or deadly.

9. It's a good rule to keep a list of _____ phone numbers to use in case a problem arises.

10. To stay safe at home, _____ touch guns, even if you think they're not loaded.

Name: _____   Date: _____

FIRE SAFETY

Write the word or phrase from the box that best completes each sentence.

smoke	fire drill	flammable
fire extinguisher		smoke detector

1. There should be a _____ outside each sleeping area and at least one on every floor of a house.

2. You should never store _____ objects close to a radiator or fireplace.

3. The expiration date on a _____ tells you how long the chemicals are active.

4. If a room is filled with _____, cover your nose and mouth with a wet cloth and crawl low to the floor.

5. To help you plan your escape route in case of a fire, you can have a

   _____.

Write True or False for each statement. If false, change the underlined word or phrase to make it true.

_____ 6. Wood and plastic are common flammable materials.

_____ 7. Candles do not produce enough heat to be a hazard.

_____ 8. In case of a fire, you should try to fight the fire yourself.

_____ 9. You should activate a public fire alarm system as soon as you suspect a fire.

_____ 10. A good fire safety plan should include a meeting place outside the building.

McGraw-Hill School Division

Name: _____   Date: _____

OUTDOOR SAFETY

Here are some sentences about outdoor safety. Put a check mark in the blank beside each sentence that gives you good advice about staying safe outdoors. Then explain why each sentence is or is not good advice. Use complete sentences.

_____ **1.** If you are swimming at a lake, a good way to improve your endurance is to swim when you feel tired.

_____

_____

_____ **2.** Everyone on a boat should wear a flotation device—even the good swimmers.

_____

_____

_____ **3.** If someone is in trouble in the water, only a trained lifeguard should go into the water to try to rescue the swimmer.

_____

_____

_____

_____ **4.** The color of your clothing doesn't make any difference in hot and cold weather.

_____

_____

_____ **5.** Traffic signs and lights are intended for cars, so bike riders don't need to follow the signs that seem confusing or inconvenient.

_____

_____

Name: _____   Date: _____

EMERGENCIES AND FIRST AID

Underline the word or phrase that best completes each sentence.

1. People who are (unconscious, choking) are unaware of their surroundings.

2. An injury in which a bone is broken or cracked is a (puncture wound, fracture).

3. If a deep wound continues to bleed, you should (cover it with more bandages, remove the bandages).

4. In case of a fracture, you should use (bandages, ice) to reduce swelling.

5. To remove chemicals from a person's eyes, you should (rub vigorously with your hands, wash the eye gently with water).

6. (Paramedics, All adults) have special training in first aid and emergency medical procedures.

7. (Any trained person, Only a doctor) can help a person who is choking.

Read about each injury and tell how you would help.

8.

A boy sprains his ankle.

_____

_____

_____

9.

A man bruises his knee.

_____

_____

_____

_____

10.

A girl gets stung by a bee.

_____

_____

_____

_____

Name: _____   Date: _____

COMMUNITY HEALTH CARE

Write the word or phrase from the box that best completes each sentence.

clinic	hospice	nurse	paramedic	pediatrician

pharmacist   physical therapist   physician assistant

1. A person who prepares medicines according to a doctor's orders is a

   _____ .

2. A doctor who takes care of babies is a _____ .

3. In a _____ you get medical treatment at little cost.

4. A person who might perform a medical procedure on you, under your
   doctor's supervision, is a _____ .

5. You might work with a _____ if you injure a leg or other
   part of your body and need help recovering.

6. A person who is very ill or dying might go to a _____ .

7. In a medical emergency, a _____ might assist a person in
   an ambulance on the way to a hospital.

8. If you're sick or injured, the person who might take care of you or assist
   your doctor is a _____ .

Answer each question in complete sentences.

9. What is the purpose of a community immunization program?

   _____

   _____

10. What is the difference between an inpatient and an outpatient?

   _____

   _____

Name: _____ Date: _____

PUBLIC HEALTH LAWS AND SERVICES

Complete each sentence with a word or phrase that makes the sentence true.

1. Garbage collection is one aspect of public _____ that is regulated in most communities.

2. Health department inspectors check restaurants and food stores to make sure the owners are following _____.

3. To protect your heath, your drinking water is checked for _____.

4. Many communities have laws that forbid _____ in public places to protect people from the harmful effects of passive smoke.

5. In a crisis, such as an earthquake or a _____, the government or private groups may offer disaster relief.

6. You can look in the phonebook to find a _____ number to call in a crisis.

Write True or False for each statement. If the statement is false, change the underlined word or phrase to make it true.

_____ 7. One way to help keep your community underline{messy} is by recycling.

_____ 8. Another way to help keep your community healthy is by underline{using} household products that contain harmful chemicals.

_____ 9. To ask for help in an emergency, a underline{community hot line} is a good place to call.

_____ 10. Disaster underline{relief} is the support that is given to people in time of crises.

Name: _____   Date: _____

AIR AND NOISE POLLUTION

Write the word or phrase from the box that best completes each sentence.

asbestos	carbon monoxide	lead	smog	soot

1. A substance found in exhaust from vehicles that causes damage to the nervous system is _____.

2. A pollutant produced by wood-burning stoves and exhaust from some factories is _____.

3. A combination of smoke, fog, and exhaust that you may not be able to see is _____.

4. Insulation in some buildings contains _____, which scars lungs and can cause cancer.

5. An air pollutant that reduces the oxygen level in the blood is _____.

Underline the phrase that best completes each sentence.

6. In emphysema, the (alveoli, tumors) of the lungs are damaged, making it difficult to take in oxygen.

7. The ozone layer protects the earth from (harmful rays from the sun, exhaust from wood-burning stoves).

8. Long-term exposure to loud noise can damage the (bronchial tubes, nerve cells) in your ears.

9. The higher the decibel level, the (louder, softer) the sound.

10. Living in a noisy environment can (lower your ability to concentrate, raise the level of smog in your community).

McGraw-Hill School Division

Name: _____   Date: _____

LAND AND WATER POLLUTION

Identify the source of water or land pollution shown in each picture.

1.
_____

2.
_____

3.
_____

4.
_____

Underline the word or phrase that best completes each sentence.

5. To reduce the threat of toxic wastes, wastes are dumped and buried in (groundwater, a landfill).

6. One way to dispose of wastes is to burn them in (an incinerator, a recycling center).

7. In a water treatment plant, (a pesticide, chlorine) is used to kill bacteria.

8. When you don't buy products with unnecessary packaging, you are (reusing, reducing) wastes.

9. Two natural resources are (water and forests, acids and plastics).

10. To spread the word about pollution to other people, suggest that they (throw away all glass and metal items, find other uses for discarded items).